Gunpowder and Tea

by Lisa Moore

illustrated by Mou-sien Tseng

 HOUGHTON MIFFLIN   BOSTON

Wen Do trudges along the vast stretch of dirt and dry grass. The two pails weigh heavily, full of tea, but Wen Do's back is strong. His job is to haul the water, boil it, and brew the tea, a special Chinese tea called *sencha*. Wen Do's father says he is the most essential person on the gang. "Without you, there is no tea, and if there is no tea," he smiles through his thin beard, "there is no work."

The sturdy bamboo pole balances across Wen Do's shoulders. Not one drop spills as he lumbers to the edge of the woods where the men are digging out stumps.

It is the summer of 1865, and these men are clearing the way for the first transcontinental railroad to stretch across the United States from the Atlantic Ocean to the Pacific, linking the nation from coast to coast. Many people feel that this railroad will transform the United States by enabling people to ship goods faster and cheaper than before. To speed its progress, two companies have devised a race to a point in Utah. Daily, the newspapers report on each company's progress. The whole country is riveted by tales of the building of the transcontinental railroad.

Wen Do and his father work for the Central Pacific Railroad Company. This company is building its part of the railroad in Sacramento and working its way east. Another company, the Union Pacific, is building in the east and working its way west. The Central Pacific faces challenges that the Union Pacific will never face: the rugged canyons, gorges, summits, and cliffs of the Sierra Nevada and Rocky Mountains. Any one of these challenges can stop them, but the determined leaders of the Central Pacific refuse to lose this race. They are prepared to do anything to win.

One strategy is to recruit Chinese workers to help them build the railroad. The Chinese are hard workers, labor for less money, and are willing to take risks.

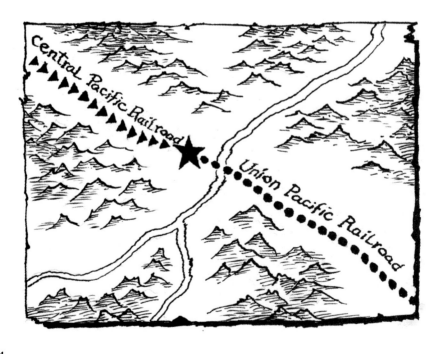

Wen Do stops before a wooden barrel that is half full of weak, tepid tea and fills it from his two pails. Now, a young man approaches and fills his cup from the spigot. Wen Do watches the man's throat rise and fall as he swallows. The man walks away without talking or acknowledging Wen Do. His rudeness fills Wen Do with longing for home. It seems like an eternity since he left China, but it has been little more than a year. Wen Do thinks about China as he continues working. Life was very different in China. It still amazes Wen Do that a simple conversation with an old friend of his father's led them to this place.

In China, Wen Do's family were farmers who worked a small plot of land outside the city of Shanghai. Each week his father would load up the wagon and drive the tired oxen into the city, hoping to sell their meager crops. Times were hard in China. Rain had been scarce and the crops had suffered. Like other farmers, Wen Do's father grew rice, which required wet fields in which to flourish. The lack of rain was hurting all the local farmers, who shared a growing fear that the dry spell would become a drought.

Everyone in the family had to work in the fields to help raise the crops. Wen Do had dreamed of becoming a teacher, but with the harsh growing season, there would be no money for additional schooling. So Wen Do had put his books aside and worked the land, as his ancestors had before him. As he labored, he watched his mother grow old and his sister's beautiful hands become coarse as they worked beside him.

Each night, Wen Do and his family prayed to their ancestors, lighting incense and placing offerings at an altar. But it seemed as if the old ones had turned a deaf ear to the family's pleas. Day after day, the harsh sun beat down on the wilting rice fields. The trips to the Shanghai market became less frequent since there was less and less rice to sell.

Then one day, a chance conversation changed their lives. It happened on a market day. After struggling for two weeks, Wen Do and his father decided that they had enough rice to sell. They began the slow walk from their small village to Shanghai.

For the first time in days, Wen Do heard his father sing. Wen Do emulated his father's good mood and banished all bad thoughts.

On their way, Wen Do found a piece of red silk along the road. "Guard it well," said his father. "It is a sign of good fortune."

Wen Do quickly folded the red silk and hid it in his clothes. So it was that in high spirits, he and his father entered Shanghai.

Wen Do and his father met with the local rice merchant. He looked carefully over their rice and then began to barter with Wen Do's father. The two men haggled over the price but finally came to an agreement. The rice merchant handed Wen Do's father the money. Now it was time for Wen Do and his father to relax a little before they began the long journey home.

Strolling through the market, they admired the burnished hanging ducks, the many colorful rolls of cloth, and the wide array of other trinkets for sale. Suddenly an older man clapped Wen Do's father on the back. Father and son turned to see the venerable Mr. Hun smiling at them.

"So nice to see you!" said Mr. Hun, laughing. Wen Do and his father bowed in greeting.

"It is good, indeed," said Mr. Hun. "Let me buy you one of these nice buns—see, they are hot and filled with egg! Or perhaps some sticky rice with pickles?"

"Yes, fine, thank you," said Wen Do and his father. "Whatever you wish to share." With a flourish, Mr. Hun purchased both treats, and the three found a quiet, shady spot where they could eat.

As they munched their food, Mr. Hun regaled Wen Do and his father with tales of his elder son's exploits in the faraway United States where his son was working to build a railroad. "He has such an important job," Mr. Hun said with pride. "And for his hard work, he makes much money."

Wen Do and his father nodded at Mr. Hun and told him that they wished his son continued good fortune and much happiness. As the men prepared to depart and go their separate ways, Mr. Hun said quietly, "This railroad company—it is looking for more workers." He smiled benignly, as if he were the Emperor himself, bestowing a wonderful wish on Wen Do's father.

"Perhaps you yourself would like to secure employment working on the railroad."

"I would consider it an honor to discuss this possibility," replied Wen Do's father.

"Then I will give you the name of a man—right here in Shanghai—who can tell you more," said Mr. Hun. Before Wen Do's father could change his mind, Mr. Hun gave him a name and address and disappeared.

Wen Do felt as if their fate had suddenly been sealed, for his father could not lose face with Mr. Hun. He swallowed hard, wondering what would happen now. Their journey home was silent as they considered their future.

At home, Wen Do's father and mother discussed whether they should go to the United States. They reflected on how prosperous Mr. Hun looked. They concluded that his son must indeed be doing well in order to send so much money home to his father. Finally, they decided that Wen Do and his father would go to the United States.

That night the family had a fine meal of duck, rice, and fish to celebrate their decision. "I will ask my brother to move here and work the farm," said Wen Do's father. His brother had two sons who needed work. In this way, Wen Do's mother and sister would be provided for while the two men made their way to the United States. "In America, we will work hard, and save money to come home. We can send Wen Do back to school!" Perhaps Wen Do's father would even buy a shop—and they would have a dowry for Wen Do's sister, too. They concluded that good luck must have been smiling on them when they met Mr. Hun in the marketplace.

Then Wen Do remembered the red silk and tried to give it to his mother. But she insisted that he keep it and take it with him on his journey.

One week after his uncle and cousins arrived, Wen Do and his father left for Shanghai. There, they met with a man who was recruiting workers for the railroad. Wen Do's father paid the man a fee, and the man promised them jobs. Then they traveled to Hong Kong where, a week later, the two boarded a steamer—a huge ship packed with hundreds of men. When they arrived in San Francisco, they were hired for $28 a month. They would work on the railroad, six days a week from sunrise to sunset. Wen Do's father would work building the railroad; Wen Do would be the tea boy.

Wen Do stops daydreaming about the past and picks up the heavy tea pails. Now he and his father are members of a gang of fifteen Chinese men. Wen Do's father is the headman. Once a month, the white bosses pay him for the gang's work; then he gives the cook money to order food from China. The gang eats together three times each day—dried fish, raisins, apples, tomatoes, eggs, beets, turnips, and pickles, seaweed, mushrooms, and rice. The food arrives in wooden crates, shipped in the hulls of the same boats that brought the Chinese workers. Their food supply is different from the other workers, and they must pay for it themselves, but they feel it is worth it. Eating food from China makes them feel as though they are still linked to their homeland.

After months of hard labor, the work gang—and hundreds of others like it—reach a site along the route called Cape Horn. For the next three miles, they must build the railroad along the side of a very steep mountain. Its slope is 75°—almost the steep 90° of a straight, up-and-down cliff. The American River is 1,200 to 2,200 feet below. This slope is too steep for a trail, or even a goat path. To build this stretch of railroad, they must blast a road out of the granite rocks. American engineers call the job "ridiculous" and "preposterous." To them, it seems impossible.

The Chinese men discuss and analyze the work for many nights. Carving roads that cling to mountains is an ancient art long practiced by Chinese engineers. They choose Wen Do's father to talk to the white boss, Mr. Strobridge.

"The Chinese built the Great Wall," he says, "and we can build this." The Chinese have a long tradition, using drilling and blasting skills to carve the mountains.

Mr. Strobridge is skeptical, but he agrees to let them try. "There is one thing we need," says Wen Do's father. "We need rope."

Mr. Strobridge wears a patch over one eye, the result of a blasting accident. He is six feet and one inch tall, and chomps on a fat cigar. "We'll get you all the supplies you need." Two days later, wagonloads of rope arrive at their camp.

The next morning, Wen Do rises before dawn to gather fresh water for the morning's tea. He scuttles down to the river and fills two pails. Balancing them on his strong shoulders, he begins the slow, cautious climb back up the hill. Halfway there, he carefully lays down his load, then lies on his back in the dewy grass and studies the fading stars.

Wen Do shuts his eyes and envisions a future when long shiny trains will soar along these cliffs as fast as shooting stars. He imagines trains full of excited people, people who, like him, want to see the whole world. When he opens his eyes, the sky has turned from dark blue to rosy pink. He must hurry back to camp.

The men have risen and are sipping tea, beginning their breakfast of pickled eggs and rice. When they finish, they rise in unison. The men work silently together, and it is this teamwork that allows them to work so fast and so well.

After Wen Do cleans up the campsite and brews more tea, he hoists the full pails onto his shoulders and trots to the worksite. When he gets close, he sees the ropes coiled like huge snakes. Soon, he knows, they will wind around his father and lower him down the mountain. Wen Do smiles proudly to himself: It is his father who will lead the way, setting the first, important sticks of dynamite.

He pours the tea into the barrels, sets his pails down, and approaches the edge of the rock where the men are gathered around his father.

Wen Do's father wears two long, thick ropes around his waist. As the men lower him slowly over the edge of the steep canyon, his feet bounce off the granite rock face with a dull thump.

Wen Do squints into the sun, watching his father descend. His father's body grows smaller and smaller. About fifty feet down, his father stops, swinging just a little next to the cliff. At the top, four men brace tightly, holding the two ropes attached to his father's waist.

"Go!" yells his father, and the men pull hard. Wen Do counts: *1,001, 1,002, 1,003,* and *1,004.* His father scampers up the mountain face, agile as a goat, and leaps lightly over the cliff's edge.

"Success," he says to the others. "I have chosen a spot for the drilling."

He glances over at his son. "Wen Do," he calls. "Go back for more tea. When you return, we will be ready to blast."

Wen Do runs back to the campsite, the empty pails bouncing. He throws more sticks on the fire so it will burn hot enough to boil the water. Then he pauses, remembering something hidden in his pack. The scrap of red silk.

He fingers it, then finds the bag of tea. It is old, embroidered on the outside with two dragons, face to face, one from the east, one from the west. Inside are dry tea leaves. As Wen Do touches them, they emit a fragrance like water lilies. He sprinkles a handful into the pot and pours the boiling water over them.

He lets the tea steep for a few minutes, then strains it into the two pails and covers them. As he hoists the pole onto his shoulders for the third time today, his heart pounds. In the distance, he hears a BLAST! The men are testing the black gunpowder to make sure it is dry.

Someone has moved the tea barrel closer to the blasting site. Wen Do carefully pours the tea into it, smelling the sweet aroma of the *sencha*.

Rising into the clouds is another smell: the gunpowder burning. It reminds him of fireworks in his Chinese village of Sunwui. When he first saw fireworks, he screamed and cried. His mother assured him that they were not dangerous, only beautiful. From that night on, he loved the pungent, sweet smell. Wen Do thinks of the smell as a good omen, but just in case he quietly fingers the piece of red silk for good luck.

The men are ready to lower Wen Do's father back down the face of the rock. This time, however, his father has a small canvas bag slung over his shoulder. In it is a rock drill, a tin of gunpowder, and fuses.

Wen Do's father is only five feet tall and weighs about 120 pounds. Wen Do can hear the white workers muttering behind him. How can he carry what he needs and still move fast enough? Wen Do says a silent prayer, rubs the red silk harder, and closes his eyes. In his heart, Wen Do knows his father is not a foolish man—he will not attempt something he cannot do. Besides, luck has been smiling down on them so far, and Wen Do has not noticed anything that might change their good fortune.

Just before he descends the cliff, Wen Do's father calls. "Wen Do! Please bring me a cup of tea!" Wen Do fills his own cup with tea and brings it to his father, who is already tied into the ropes. His father sips appreciatively.

"Your mother's tea," he says softly, his face suddenly growing pale. His eyes meet Wen Do's and he seems to gather strength and courage. Then Wen Do's father returns the cup to his son and gestures to a cluster of shrubs nearby. "You stand there," he says. "And be careful."

The men lower Wen Do's father down and down and down, the rope slipping through their strong brown fingers. Wen Do loses sight of all but his father's head. He hears the hammer pounding the drill into the rock and then the sound of falling pebbles and sand as his father drills the hole for the powder.

Poised above, the fourteen men look down over the edge into the silence.

"I am almost done," calls his father and the men take a step back to make room. Wen Do is on his hands and knees, holding his breath. The seconds seem like minutes as they all strain to see, four of the men holding the ropes, waiting for the signal. Somewhere near the mountain, a hawk screams. A sign of danger, thinks Wen Do.

21

22

"Go!" yells his father and the men pull, hand over hand over hand. Wen Do begins counting, *"1,001, 1,002, 1,003, 1,004, 1,005, 1,006 . . ."* In just seconds, the fuse will burn down to the end. The dynamite will explode. He is suddenly afraid that something disastrous will occur. There are stories of men who have died in such blasts.

Then his father's head appears over the top of the rock. He scrambles over the edge. With just ten seconds to spare, the men fall to the ground. BOOM! The explosion hurls pebbles and clods of dirt off the side of the mountain, as if a giant had just sneezed.

The leaves on the trees dance in the sudden wind like applause. Wen Do smiles and looks up to see a small bird fly by. Perhaps it is a nightingale. Tears of relief fill his eyes. His father is safe. If my father can perform such a courageous feat, Wen Do thinks, surely we can make it back to China.

Afterword

Inch by inch, the roadbed was blasted and carved from the granite. By the spring of 1866, the Chinese had worked tirelessly to lay the track on that three-mile stretch. It remains one of the best known achievements of the Central Pacific Railroad. One historian writes:

> What Clement planned and the Chinese made became one of the grandest sights to be seen along the entire Central Pacific line. Trains would halt there so tourists could get out of their cars to gasp and gape at the gorge and the grade.*

In 1969, a plaque was hung at the Golden Spike National Historic Site, the spot where the Union Pacific and the Central Pacific Railroad Companies finally met on May 10, 1869. It reads:

> *To commemorate the centennial of the first transcontinental railroad in America and to pay tribute to the Chinese workers of the Central Pacific Railroad whose indomitable courage made it possible.*

---

* Griswold, *Work of Giants*, p. 145, from Ambrose, *Nothing Like It in the World*